BRUTE

BRUTE

POEMS

Emily Skaja

Graywolf Press

This publication is made possible, in part, by the voters of Minnesota through a Minnesota State Arts Board Operating Support grant, thanks to a legislative appropriation from the arts and cultural heritage fund, and a grant from the Wells Fargo Foundation. Significant support has also been provided by Target, the McKnight Foundation, the Lannan Foundation, the Amazon Literary Partnership, and other generous contributions from foundations, corporations, and individuals. To these organizations and individuals we offer our heartfelt thanks.

Published by Graywolf Press
212 Third Avenue North, Suite 485
Minneapolis, Minnesota 55401

www.graywolfpress.org

Published in the United States of America
Printed in Canada

ISBN 978-1-55597-835-8

4 6 8 10 11 9 7 5 3

Library of Congress Control Number: 2018947085

Cover design: Mary Austin Speaker

Cover art: Walton Ford, *Gleipnir*. Image courtesy of Walton Ford and Paul Kasmin Gallery.

for the women in my life
& for anyone vulnerable to flight

CONTENTS

III: CIRCLE

IV: BRIGHT LANDSCAPE

BRUTE

I: MY HISTORY AS

You remember too much,
my mother said to me recently.

Why hold onto all that? And I said,
Where can I put it down?

—ANNE CARSON

MY HISTORY AS

In my history, I was bones eating paper
                    or I was paper eating bones. Semantics.

I lived in a narrow house;
                    I lived with a man who said

You fucked up your own life, who said
                    I could never love someone so heavy.

The place was brick on brick
                    with iron grates covering the windows—

rowhouse cage, South Philly. I was learning
                    how some of us are made to be carrion birds

& some of us are made to be circled.
                    Somewhere in this education

I stopped eating. Held up my hands
                    to see if my bones would glow in the dark.

My boat name could have been
                    HMS *Floating, Though Barely.*

Meanwhile I had a passion for cartography.
                    Not leaving, just coloring the maps.

I covered all the walls with white paint, whiter paint, spiraling out—
                    a weather system curling over water.

I always drew the compass rose flat.
                    I was metal-blue, I was running my mouth

like a bathtub tap. A bone picked clean of particulates.
                    Everything has some particular science.

By its nature, a vulture can't
                    be a common field crow, for instance.

Look at the wings, look at that hard
                    mouth, look at the feet.

When I tell my history, I can't leave out
                    how I hit that man in the jaw,

that I wasn't good at mercy,
                    that eating nothing but white pills & white air

made me unchartable—
                    I can't skip to the end just to say

well it was fragile & I smashed it
                    & everything's over, well now I know things

that make me unlikely.
                    What am I supposed to say: I'm *free?*

I learned to counter like a torn edge
                    frayed from the damp. That's how I left it.

Leaving the river, leaving
                    wet tracks arrowed in the brush.

BRUTE STRENGTH

Soldier for a lost cause, brute, mute woman
written out of my own story, I've been trying
to cast a searchlight over swamp-woods & parasitic ash
back to my beginning, that girlhood—
kite-wisp clouded by gun salutes & blackbirds
tearing out from under the hickories
all those fine August mornings so temporary
so gold-ringed by heat haze & where is that witch girl
unafraid of anything, flea-spangled little yard rat, runt
of no litter, queen, girl who wouldn't let a boy hit her,
girl refusing to be *It* in tag, pulling that fox hide
heavy around her like a flag? Let me look at her.
Tell her on my honor, I will set the wedding dress on fire
when I'm good & ready or she can bury me in it.

IT'S IMPOSSIBLE TO KEEP WHITE MOTHS

from flying out of my mouth.

I am 25. I paint the door blue. I go in when he tells me
                    to stay out. Next to a billboard

in Philadelphia that says *Your Message Here*,
                    I am sewn into a dress. On Broad Street, ravens

lurk on the Divine Lorraine Hotel as if to say
                    Always a corpse flower, never a bride.

Facing south, I can make myself apologize
                    for anything. My voice is thick—a shroud of bells.

But will I listen. What I hear in the dark
                    is my own blood stalking me

like a drunk boy wild on cheap gin
                    swinging his hammer

to nail a tree swallow flat to a barn door.
                    A bird is a vessel. It carries a field.

There are nights when I sleep on the couch
                    & lift macramé lace to my cheek from a hope chest.

Outside, a teenager shoots a teenager shoots a teenager.
                    The cops come to measure the street.

They ask me *What did you see?* I saw a hole in the whole of the picture.
                    When he comes home late from his fight at the bar,

I hold a cold rag steady to his knuckles. I think I can love someone
        who cares enough to bruise for me.

He touches his thumb to the corner of my mouth,
        pulls back my lip to consider my teeth.

I HAVE READ THE WHOLE MOON

In March I drop an egg hoping a bird will fly out disbelieving
science. All the manuals tell me this is a logical contract.
You commit yourself to a shell & you end up flying. Fine.
Stone after stone, I'm defacing the river of being in love with you.
True, I don't care how that sounds. I have a list
of cocoons to transform my body: Uncontrollable
Shaking. Sleep Paralysis. Dread of Eating. I'm guilty
of pretending the roads to your house are no longer roads
but deerpaths angled crooked through the marsh. Again the water
doesn't stop; it rains even when the weather is overdue: a holy
parallel. My mouth is rotted & anonymous. The bed needs oars.
I'm interested in dust but only new dust arriving unmarked
after you leave. After you leave, you leave &
thicketed in sludge I've been glued open. Self as spectacle:
Yolk Marvel. Unbird. Emily as grave pillar as salt lick as dammed up
luminous in thread. I have read the whole moon
cycle; it doesn't explain the cracks. Mercury for once
cannot be blamed. My dishes float in soap like little planets.
I drop my hands in the sink. They come up feathered.

ELEGY WITHOUT A SINGLE TREE I CAN SAVE

I've been standing all night in the woods near Necedah with your name etched in red on my tongue like a box-elder wing. Loss of life occurred at a specific hour, a certain day, we are told. No one was with you—how that weighs on me. That there can be no untwisting of the tree back into its seed. Innocent of all charges. Granted just one reprieve. Has there ever been anyone more false than I am, pretending I know which one is a white pine against white stars? Shouldn't I remember which of these is the tree you climbed, which of these you were too afraid to come down from? I think you were the first person to say *Cassiopeia* to me. As young as we were, we could not carry a ladder out here by ourselves. Alone, I watch the water move now like a clock someone is winding with a knife. I am starved for that easy taxonomy of Things Before. For the years not likely to be cut open with scissors only to find proof of disease. Black hair spooling from the lungs of each month since. You're gone & I collect fox fur by myself in every direction. You're gone & I misname the trees.

IN MARCH WHEN YOU TELL ME YOU DON'T

I walk in a straight line as a compass pulled the wrong way north.
High Priestess of the Not-Quite. Chief Dolorous. And fuck it all—
All of it. Unobserved, clement.
                          Being the one who—being the one that——
I have the problem of needing to say my history teeth-first to a body
of water—to the river, to the gutter, to the storm drain red & rushed
with leaves in dirty water on the way to your apartment maybe
I should give up the story that what I say can change it
notwithstanding one for, one against your cowardice
notwithstanding halfwinter light torn up wet-white & eyeless
& I know I should sky up birdward—I know I should circle high
until my arms are kited cramped but can I see you
plainly or at all from any height do I know how
to see you I do but I don't & I can't
find you on a March night moonless on the hill where I know you
are out walking the treeline slowly with your dog.
Tell me   if I can make the not-moon intercede—
If I can come south as a figure wearing starlings as a coat
If I can be If I can be If I can be
a tunnel either leafing or branching or——
                          If I can be If I can be If I can be

[IN DEFEAT I WAS PERFECT]

In defeat I was perfect
               the luster & the grime on me irresistible

Bright landscape with the sky blacked out

              A spectacle   I was tied into the clothesline drunk
In my defense   every arrogant green thing

              had been blooming against my directive

I remember   the light was pressing me down toward myself
             the trees were thick with insects

dark birds shadowed the street

             I had been circling hungry red & narrow not
slogging through the mud

             like the Magellan of any promised thing

He was leaving in arrows   he walked out
             in a boldfaced lie   I said *You need to consider me*

Consider all that   considering the future

             I had thrown into orbit
There was a truck piled neatly with boxes

He had a splintered voice that he hid from me

Is it giving up if you give what you have
                     & the universe still fucks you

Now I can't picture his face anymore   only leaves

                I remember I was desperate to speak
to expose the right language

                Understand he kept driving back to me

& back to me   He said *I didn't always*
                love you   He said *I didn't want to tell you*

to wait for me   (But wait for me)

ELEGY WITH A SHIT-BROWN RIVER RUNNING THROUGH IT

Never have I ever let anyone skin me alive for my secrets. I grow true to seed. Unfamiliar with traditions of marksmanship. Whose grouse it is. Whose grouse I am after I fall. In this hayfield I say nothing at all to the hornets. I admire their mud huts. I think only in lists. The Time I Told You to Give Up Smoking. The Time I Believed You Would Live to Be Older Than Seventeen. When I think about all the ways there are to die. By falling ice. In a coat-check. With a gallon of ethanol stale in your gut. I am dizzy. I am missing your way of blinking at me in the sun. Bus tickets seep out of my pockets. By the river I drop a tree branch shaped like a tibia. In the center of my hand is a hole. I am used to it. Of course there is shouting. There is nothing I can get behind less than drunk huntsmen observing male rituals with gusto. I would rather look at the river through the burned-out circle of my hand. Somewhere in here is a fish with a hook in its mouth—I'm sure of it.

PHILADELPHIA

—city of hot pavement

        addressed by hot pavement,

boiling puddles studded

with floating syringes, paper kites.

    A bridge swung over the water

        with direction, like a fist.

    All the time he was trying to show me

how he was a stuck door

    with an eyehole punched through

        where I saw only

    gashes of light.

Brute. He locked me out.

    I walked 3rd Street

        all the way north.

    The day's interminable heat.

Sweat tore up my thighs.

    Cherry trees, I remember,

        were blooming

    shamefully.

It was a house I was always

    walking back to.

I wasn't delicate.

The door was blue.

So it was

that the palm of my hand

held a red bruise

shaped like a bird.

A lit crow. Flamed.

How sharp it is

to be wrong-fledged.

To be rope ravel

winging out

of syncopation.

Tried trying.

Just once I wanted

to hit & hold the person

who could hit & hold

me down.

I wanted the bruise

& the voice that was sorry.

Terror to give up control—

terror to name it.

There was a bottle.

There was a bottleneck exit.

THE BRUTE / BRUTE HEART

After Pennsylvania, I couldn't breathe.
—LUCIE BROCK-BROIDO

The facts are: I drove all night through the mountains
to get away from him
I cut up my credit cards to prove I would not leave him
I woke up in the hospital
to bonesaw / brushfire / thralldom
the pieces were out of order there was glass in my cheek
I tried to swallow an entire bottle I tried to leave
without giving away my name I was not lost
I listed no forwarding address
There was a reason why I named the dog *Valor*

If I was silent I'd learned the virtue
of protecting my mouth at least
I was going home
to the house between the cemeteries
to the redbud the willow trees
the heavy muck-wet woods
I loved & in my absence
the house had been torn down
to make more space
for the dead

I stood there breathing
It felt like
sliding a hand through loose dirt looking
for tendrils & pockets of air
It's easy to be angry
about how much hope there is
in reaching
The whole house gone

& so many little monuments
to the wrong thing

In the bare yard
all of my good trees
still framed the hole
where the house had been standing
In my new life whatever I claimed
I didn't feel it was *mine*
How easily I could be a river dragged
a gray car raised up from the bottom dripping
Already I was on a string I could be lurched up
out of hiding & the evidence tagged

He took the money he said I made him crazy it was my fault
What was wrong with me how could I ever think
I could leave was I really so stupid he said
he would call the police
he set my furniture on fire he said
he would drive my dog to the pound if I went out
I'd like to say now that he was just a list of grievances
Who else would try so hard on someone so fucking worthless
is some kind of war proposal
that no longer works on me

What I want is a permanent figure
I want a marker here to separate
The Time Before from The Time Now
One ivied-over angel
for a woman with no known name & no known history
A monument for the disappearance of X
for the opening of a deep well in which I would tread water
for the blood to tide
for the trees to fall
for 100 years of winter

II: GIRL SAINTS

To assess the damage is a dangerous act.

—CHERRÍE MORAGA

GIRL SAINTS

O LORD, when the Angel said *Listen*
when the Angel said *Do not fall to the earth for anyone*

we were already stained in glass.

A circle of black flies biting
our arrival. Scales scraped off of a fish.

Starved girls folded at a line from Leviticus.

This is how it happened: one day we looked outside
& the bloated bodies of frogs were fucking up the yard.

Our hands bled. We saw Rorschach blood in our wounds,

Pietà in egg yolks. There was a hope chest & a threshold
& a bridegroom—revoltingly pagan. We said

Bring us the coat-check ticket for our eyes.

Nothing was so underpaid as our attention.
If ghost, if whore, if virgin—same origin story:

because X was a face too lovely, Y was a corpse in the lake.

Our sisters said *Wait.* Our mothers said *Stay the hell awake.*
We bled on our white clothes—we bore them redly

to the table. Our fathers said *Tell me, will you ever*

feed me something that isn't your own trouble?
We cast away stones. There was room at the inn.

There was time to be floated as witches.

When night came, an egg-moon slid over the steeple.
We stared at the blue yolk yawning in the fire.

Our Father. Who Art in Heaven.

There were men in the alley. We knew them by name.
They said they wanted to prove we were holy.

Your Angel said *Listen*—

There are not vultures enough
in this world, there are not crows

to shoot out of the sky in a shaking black line.

Please, we've been trying
to say out loud the words for this—

to see You write it out red

in a fish-hooked curve. Have mercy—
Mouth of Poison Flowers: Speak.

Mouth of Asphodel—*Say it.*

DEAR KATIE

Understand I need these fragments. To tell it once is not enough.
        I have a hundred holy objects, everything looked upon, to break.

Time will pass, time will pass me, attaching mile-marker threats

        to every causeway. I know it's useless. I put on every eyeliner I own.
I draw the shape—a different eye to see this. I map the innocent

        spill of color to my ear. Look, I'm already half an emerald. Lit & limited, I'm

cut. Now that I can't unsmudge the lines for any reason, I am difficult.
        He takes the high road; I take the thornhedge.

Katie, I can't find a way to talk about this

        but it always happens: I have no standing with the men in my life.
You are the only one who ever asks me *Are you eating?*

        Come close, too close, get out—it's a blunt-edged system

& when did I begin to choose this type of man who loves to "protect" me
        from himself? Lately, I hold your name in my mouth

like a talisman because we are never afraid of the same things.

        Remember the dead dog we found on the bridge road. *A coyote*, I said.
Raised as I was near a cemetery, I always assume some authority

        over the departed. Stray magic. Lies about the natural world

comfort me, I admit. Like if a tree feels something
        when another tree is fucking up her life. I believe in patterns. Shapes.

Pinnate, whorled. I remember too the accordion doors of the Blue Line train

       & the way it spit me out piss-drunk on the O'Hare platform crying
because I wasn't sure if I'd hit him or if I'd only wanted to.

       I was trying to starve myself out of a feeling. Signals & timelines.

& if the train comes out of the tunnel before I count to ten
       then I'm not the most fucked thing. & if not, then when.

My own mouth bleeding is a nice round number.

       On your couch I fall asleep with puke in my hair & I dream
that I'm trapped in a water tower. *Katie,* I wake up saying.

ELEGY WITH FEATHERS

When you're gone I press my hand to the stove just once. Patches of blisters pearl on my palm. I have sense enough to put on my coat. On the boat I am called Red. I take every other phrase from an elocution book. I wear a high collar that rubs against my cheek & in the rain it leaves a scratch raised like a welt. I pretend not to know why you're gone, pretend there is not the same sickness inside me. I try to explain about the curse for which the cure is not thinking. On the fourth day, notes on a disaster include water & water. A man on the boat follows me all day, *just one question then I'll leave you alone.* There is nowhere a girl can go that a man like this won't have a question. A trade he feels owed. There's a hole in his glove & the skin underneath is peeled raw. A teakettle boils on the wind. *Help me.* On my knees I ask to be turned into a gull. I shift into white gloss, feathers.

DEAR RUTH

Anyone can be a plank-mouthed bird or anyone can be the sky hallelujah
is the accepted lie of hymns. Like a girl walking has never needed to fly

but could if she wanted. If winged & if the wings fit—if fielded, if felt.
What is the difference between asking & asking for it are the words

that we should burn into a field, *Oh Glory.* Whether you are lost
or whether you are the blondest bird leaned against a fence

hemming in an orchard, Ruth, you are the holy thing I look to.
So explain to me about the habits of cicadas, why only the men

speak, why it takes some of them 17 years to come correct.
All the leaves are eaten bare; yet the tree is not empty, we know

from experience—*Ecclesiastes.* Help me understand, help me reverse
the pilgrims' stories. Make them rise up out of their bone crypts

doubled with purpose—bloodied, believing—& send them to war
for their girl queens. War for their daughters hallelujah

*as it wasn't in the beginning isn't now & never shall be
world without end.* Oh but God my God *Amen.*

[IT WASN'T ABOUT LOVE]

It wasn't about love   I was giving a speech

I was saying *This is about violence*

Get over love, sure   Bright landscape

It was a house that fell down   I fell toward myself

I couldn't see myself at the bottom I woke up on the dirt floor of the old cellar I had new limbs

New inadequate gestures of suffering   Chimeric thing

Blurred reaching   wings out

pelican mouth   unfull but full of loathing

Would you describe that sound as wailing?

I was speaking   I said *I never want to survive that story again*

It was explained to me that I was in danger

Someone was listening

If you say X then we'll have to tell someone

I was speaking   I didn't say X

I said yes to a bottle I said yes

to the rope of my own hands

to a body to a body

                          I was only   I was only

A body alone with its own blood   blue

                              in its skin-tape

ELEGY WITH SYMPTOMS

Under cover of darkness, I consider the alternatives. High water. Firing squad. Infirmary. I'm angry with you for leaving me no particular method. Please note I am not giving up yet on the cliff road. What happens to a woman at 19 at 25 at 29 can make her vulnerable to flight. First the tripwires drop away from my fingers. Next I'm learning the names for the parts of a bell. Eggs crack. A chalk line darts up my arm. Here I am as a hairpin curve. Here I am as cyanide stowed away in an apple seed. I am looking for lost arrows. Girl tribes of the hinterland. For scales to fall away from the eyes of anything, anything. *Please.* I have learned the way rain rots thick in a barrel. Given the relevant texts, I am dangerous. Around me, black bats dive up in the dark. I've been wrong, I've been trying to pry off the planks from these windows. I am keeping the box that I came in. I am keeping my wrong blood—look at it vine through my wrist like a brand.

INDICTMENT

Didn't I tell you & didn't I tell you Emily

               not to fight for the gospel of error

not to row out as far as the river goes

               not to raise up your arms like a waxwing bird

like you're free, like you're everything

               falling? You fall like it's your fault,

like you know how to breathe

               under milfoil & reeds. You look

like you're already drowning

               in air. You don't know

& you don't know & isn't that Emily

               the shape of it? A braided rope

becomes a ladder you can climb

               into a hole. Underneath

every pattern is a logic

               it's your privilege to ignore

& yours is dreamsense yours is erasure

Hello you

are a vessel of vessels.

Hold your wings like the oars of a boat.

Don't tell me the sun is an exit

the sky is a clamp.

LETTER TO S, HOSPITAL

Does it take a fever to recognize a fever
Is it true that you can't love a man

Against his will & get away
Without a scratch

Tell me when did I know
Was I dull vapor   hoarse light

Was I walking damp with fog through a stand of pines
Forgive me I've been sick

I was so sick
With belonging

I wanted to keep my mouth shut
Loyally

I wanted girlhood circled around me
Like a coat

You said *You should apologize* I should have
Wanted to be saved

For worse I needed to peel my own paint
Miranda my own arrest

RULES FOR A BODY COMING OUT OF WATER

In a story, a girl is a tree / is a bird / is a wilderness.
      A girl wakes up underwater, nail by nail builds herself

the same wooden raft, eats the mulberries & the blackberries
      set out for the trap & she gets away from him

somehow, the price a piece of herself.
      Compromised by longing & looking for language

to note the differences in the map: the pointed spruces
      tipped against the moon this time

& the water halflit, star-slid—but it makes no difference
      in the telling. The story is familiar

& she has been told what she can expect from men.
      Because the body is incorrect. The body is fragile

in tar & marline, skin written over with shame
      like a register of witch-burning. So the body is stubborn:

spalted pith of one lung falters, lumbers open.
      Air, dirt air. When fingers reach for fox sedge, claw

for rushes, the air rushes up to meet her grassward.
      So the body is inventory—shunt.

Clutch of hair like a root looping back on itself.
      Her hair is juniper rope.

I'm asking: how can she get at the start of this place?
      Blue river nameless, sky blank, pointless

code of moss—if she's traveling north now,
        true north, north to what?

I can say *our voice is a burned voice*
        but she doesn't know the way back

after the pigeons have eaten the words
        I dredged with flour & left to rise.

DEAR EMILY

Easy to disown the girl you were
at 23: fluffed dove-gray

& bridal, eyes up, prim bird claws
pink on the brute arm

of your first wreck,
your original lesson

in leaving a fire
to burn itself to ash.

With him you were cob-eyed,
blind-cut—a tin girl

ridged & perfect,
yawning flora,

all vinegar
hysteria & brine.

So you dreamed
that he drowned

you. You dreamed of blue
floodwater mold,

the traps he set
wire by hook.

You waited for hail,
a plague of swollen fish

to sting his mouth
before you slapped him,

before he told you
You're the one

who ruined your life.
You knew

all the reasons,
the ledgers, the birds

caught in windows,
your hands flaking rust—

tin girl clutching what,
holding what

to hide your nakedness?
Give her up now, that girl

who can't be you,
who can't be anyone

flung over his bed
like a sheet.

III: CIRCLE

Every woman adores a Fascist,
The boot in the face, the brute
Brute heart of a brute like you.

—SYLVIA PLATH

AUBADE WITH BOUNDARIES

You think you can choose to remember our story
                        however you want it. That you can run up your flag

& say *True Love Lost* & we're even.

Even the whiskey, even the salt we licked from the table
                        won't return us to our roles of wanted & wanting.

                In an argument, it is better to be drunk than to be right.

When you screamed at me *You don't know everything about me*
                        there was snow melting on my hair;

                we were blackout drunk in a ladies' toilet.

Black sharpie under the mirror commanded me
                        UNFUCK YOUR HOLE LIFE.

                I couldn't stop drying my hands. I was saying *I'm sorry*

but my mouth was obsessed with the word *precedent.*
                        Girls are taught that adage early: *To permit it gives permission.*

                How many implements of shame should I hold against

myself? Blight, motherfucker,
                        is the introduction of a bruise down one thigh.

                Now I've learned to say *remember* like memory is not

the axis on which the world shifts
                        & interplanetary garbage is not, like, just drifting.

Go back & go back & go back to the beginning is useless.

I can't remember the chemicals for choking roaches
                    & the roaches are everywhere.

        Orange light slides over the railyard

where I watch the workers circle the tracks.
                  They replace one empty traincar with another.

FOUR HAWKS

circle the same mile of Indiana where I force myself to look

at every dead deer on the road, as if that braces me, as if I believe
it will protect me from losing anything good.

I can't stop dreaming I'm hiding

my own prints in the snow, convinced
my mouth is a metal trap, a part of it, apart

from you, & when you pull me awake
it's because I'm lining my body with burrs,

because I'm antlers & talons & I know

the smell of cedar is home, is a ring of sky
I love, but I can't take it when

you say *Only deer, only hawks.*

Why is there nothing wild in you
to explain it, nothing killing; why

am I the chased thing horrified
to overtake myself in the brush I wonder &

if a deer darts across this road & the dead don't
take it, don't the dead wait, don't I know,

don't the dead always covet something running?

I count bodies like cold days in March.

Ten, eleven, twelve—& you
with the map unfolded, following the sky.

I wonder if you & I are twin limbs
of something running.

If you & I circle.

HOW TO MEND A FAUCET DRIPPING THREAD

You are in Nepal, maybe dreaming of astronauts.

Every morning, a spider webs over my door, but I don't do omens.
I refuse to weave. I am not Penelope.

I will not hang all the maids, for example; it's antifeminist.
But I will lie here with my face annexing the floor. *Penelope, neat.*
Pouring out a little whiskey for the sirens & swine.

From the bathtub I will drunk-direct an orchestra
of boring nebulae. Leading the scales
major-minor minor-minor.

We observe the moon at opposite intervals.

By now you've seen my constellation, the jaw of a wolf.
Can you tell that the stars are on fire with longing?
Every tooth is there—my right mind stitched.

Or else the moon is taped up for the solstice. Comma
how are you. What with the leeches.

I don't think anyone was expecting a supermoon to fly.
For instance, a person knows not
to surrender the absence of space, & gravity

calls us. The moon is still & the night is forked
when I pull months straight out of the tap.

& I know, I get it—I'm counting the ship sails
holey with mothbite. I know about drowning, fine.

My mind is a wishbone drying. I hold it taut & pull to break.

ELEGY WITH BLACK SMOKE

Three notes: long, long, short—your call for me. In a prism of light I walk backward. I see a house turn into a bull turn into a house. I shake myself, wincing. I hold onto the facts. You've been dead eighteen years. The house was torn down for the cemetery. A man on the mill road stops me for my papers. I don't say *I woke up in a red pond & my arms are made of magnets.* Whole cities follow me south. I can't help it; I drag them behind me. When I'm not careful, worms appear on the road & I waste an entire rainstorm sobbing. I don't tell anyone the code words stuck to my coat. Without you, all the proverbs are halved in my mouth. *Where there's smoke there's.* Where there's smoke.

[FOR DAYS I WAS SILENT]

For days I was silent——If he had called me I would have gone back
               on every promise I made to myself——

But there had to be a move toward withdrawal——Those were the rules——
               Before I was ready——No one could come in & unharm me

Rebecca said *Don't ever let anyone fucking tell you how to manage your grief*——
               There was blood under my fingernails——*Your blood* she clarified

I couldn't keep anything down——Or anything uncontaminated——At the time I
               had one recurring nightmare——Dead locusts under my feet——

A casket budding empty——Hanging there——Turning in oak root——
               What was the nature of the threat he made to you

Planet with no name——Tell me——
               At what point could I have been trusted——

Not to let him into the house——Not to repeat his words
               back to him——One by one in a pattern——

When I have lived through this——I wanted to ask——
               When I am full-alive untied from him——

Will I be required——*To haul out into the sun & let burn dry*
               the blood I lost——*On each of these estrangements*——*Will I?*

There I am——Pictured with my face obscured
               Bright landscape——With my arms bleeding out of the picture——

ELEGY FOR R

I'm inventing a way
to speak to you.
To explain

the way it felt—
like 50 acres
burning.

Spruce, pine,
fir. Everything
ashes.

Like we dug ditches
all night
to save them.

If I don't believe
there is a collective
cloud space

I believe
there is something
in trees

& I learned grief
spares nothing—
maple, cedar, hemlock

ditchline black
with treefire
treecinder treefall—

our mouths
filled with dirt,
the woods

loud
with what chaos
survived it.

It's the first year
you've been dead longer
than you were ever

alive. What
would you say
about that?

I was 10—
I looked up *suicide*
in the dictionary—

I didn't know
anything. Without
you, we were

heavy, divided.
We knelt down
in the dirt

where the roots
were suspended
in water.

[REMARKABLE THE LITTER OF BIRDS]

Remarkable the litter of birds cleared from the city every morning
The ones who flew toward the sky in the reflection of the glass
Dead or stunned I often think given the chance I wouldn't live my life over
I have just this one heart okay I was burned I was gaslit nearly to ash on the first try
From the start I was told I was a powerful speaker I was told when & how I should speak
It's true I made a feast of my own misery I invited everyone the whole gang
We ate only flowers it was my misery after all I was 29
I'd had a narrow escape from becoming Julian of Norwich
Finally I felt safe enough to ask Katie *Is it antifeminist to starve myself over a boy?*
Her response was kind *What if we revise the focus of that question*
Soon we were eating peonies & lilacs with bees inside
All these marriages had come out to watch me deliver my speech
I filled my mouth with bees I tried to speak through the bees
Everyone if we're going to talk about love please we have to talk about violence
I was stung my tongue swelled I was spitting crushed bees
A special crew came to sweep them up before anyone could see

SELF-PORTRAIT WITH HAWK & ARMADA

Oh hawk after hawk over Indiana—
                    are you watching me
break up on bed after white bed sobbing,
        doing all the dishes

except the one his mouth touched,
                    burying my grief
in the thaw-wet yard,
            turning mud into water miraculous?

What are you here to collect?
                    Spring, I can see, is in full effect
allowing grass-reeds-wild-river-
        birch-flood-plains & even robins

are compelled by the way *this*
                    broke the hell out of *that's* ripped heart.
Slow. I'm taking it with Ecclesiastes.
        A time for a time for a time.

Yes, hawk, the winter was disappointing,
                    but we've left scraps.
Beetles have arrived like shorn locusts
        shedding what I remember

of the summer when the trees buzzed with wings & shells
                    the leaves alive / alive
it leaves the problem of remembering
        without erasing it—

for all of March I've felt the water rising
                    & I've measured what I knew.

Oh hawk, what's your damage—
        are you here to pick the bones

of the years I laid waste to
                like I never loved a thing? So be it.
I see the beetles march across the linoleum
        & I let them.

Can't feed young trees to the chipper
                can't suck the dirt out of my nails
but I can stand here reciting all the words I have
        over the hole & that's what's left—

Done with the whole dark
           & the insect dirge
under blue lit lamps.
        Done trying to remember

June, first stars & August
           when I was Penelope
when I was Eurydice
        when July was missing

& I was my own dull shade.
            Listen to me, I'm not hiding it—
I'm swimming out to meet the boats
        coming armed up the river

& I wish he were watching
           through a lead-black fog.
I had his book of exits learned by heart.
        I thought I knew it.

MARCH IS MARCH

We go on forward. I go on floating my face
in a map of Lake Michigan, blue there

as logically as anywhere else. When he leaves I stop

washing the cups; I stop cleaning the floors.
I don't have the patience to identify whether dirt is different

in the hue of his absence, if there is less of it,

if it possesses a graver, more articulate
sense of itself, grown worldly in suffering.

Water lurks in the drain like it's gawking.

My mother says *Why not date yourself for a while.*
Accordingly, I listen to all seven Harry Potters.

I go for long walks in a circle & insult Scalia on facebook

because I'm trying to win me over & these are my interests.
The radio is a dick to me. Pop songs are barbed with revelations

that make the people who listen to pop songs return

with a change of heart. *Rihanna*, I tweet. *I need you to be okay
& not okay at the same time as me, together in a cycle.*

I adopt a dog I keep as my shadow.

Every morning she cries when I leave & I think *Finally someone gets it.*
I force myself to take time like a pill that stops my pulse

but just for a minute. Time collects around 4:30, refusing to move.

I leave the dog for an hour & she chews up
her bed, a blue blanket, her cage door

& I say *You can't keep doing this—*

& I say *What am I supposed to do—*
& I say *You don't understand*

I need to leave you EVERY DAY I need to leave.

THANK YOU WHEN I'M AN AXE

I was a list   a rainy incident   an axe   & a pact with contagion.
Autobiography: *storm*   *thunderstorm*   *tornado*   *November.*

Yes, all of the major stages are rendered in code.

On the left, an emotional field.
                                        On the right, ho hum, some circuitry.

Remember when I was a young axe
making promise after promise to the young trees?

Stump speech in the mode of hypothesis. Bravado. Cue to the fall.

When I lay flat on the floor with him & said
                                A relationship doesn't end with one person running.

I am not about to die loosely jacketed among the burr oaks.
Together it's dark-starved chlorophyll burning. Tell him to pick

me up. If I say marrow, if I say caught.
If I love cedar & thistle & curve,   I'll keep it so quiet.

November is wood-notch, frozen dirt, rain.
                                I'm working for light. I'm bleeding for lightness.

Society of the tomahawk, I defend my speech
on the nature of secrets.   I marry mine to a yoke.

I want to know if two years are the measure.
What they are the measure of.   Cut once.

If a woodpile is reason when brambling.

If the dark if the dark if the dark.

Thank you for doubting me so I swung hard.

IV: BRIGHT LANDSCAPE

hell must break before I am lost;

before I am lost,
hell must open like a red rose
for the dead to pass.

—H.D.

NO, I DO NOT WANT TO CONNECT WITH YOU ON LINKEDIN

Of all the washed-up terror prodigies in all the Underworld——
I need you especially to stay the fuck out of my iPhone.

So you're still king of that shot-up little roach house on Cat Piss Ave,

still hung up on that time I didn't let you stay my dearest
threat? Look at you. So mad you'd @ anything.

Wanting me taken down, taken out. Lolol, rage-cake. You *tried*.

In the years since I was last light-starved, hell-bent on your half-cocked lure,
I have kept the moon on all night in my own way,

by listening, by not forgetting it is there. Small witchery.

And by the way, your shit is not a secret. This here is girl country.
Trust me when I say we know *all about* your kind in our ranks.

All you motherfuckers make it easy—you wear the same shitty face.

Rude to the end, you missed my victory scene. I wore blue lace
& wolf spit, I sang torch songs, I was carried up into the trees by waves.

The moon knew me. It took my side. *Duh*, I thought & I gave you the finger.

One day, I woke up such a force, I watched your name fall
right out of the language. Did you feel that?

How you are now girl dust? Shipwreck? Bone muck? *Ghost?*

It's only in another life that I could be damned
back to hell for your half-look, that I was

                                        ever your jilted bride, sweating it out

Aqua-Netted in a farm field down by the interstate
under a goddamn willow bower, eye-deep

                                        in a rabble of no-account drunks.

You once thought to make me afraid, to consider
what that might do to me. I think now:

                                        how unimaginative. To kill a tree, any asshole

can hammer a ring of nails into the trunk.
Already, you don't know me & one day

                                        I will be even stranger, one day I just may fall

to my knees in church to say *Reverend, my God, what
were Eve's other choices* & I trust you will not

                                        be there as my witness. I admit I once believed

I could be anything, & didn't you say to me then "That's true
for some people"—? When I was 7, a boy slapped me

                                        & *I* was punished for "inciting violence."

So it began: when I bled, I thought I deserved it.
I wanted one brightly colored warship; I wanted

                                        a grief with my name printed right there on it.

To have & to hold—there is, after all, a difference.
Before anyone fucked with her, Eurydice was just a woman walking alone

                                        through a field of snakes. It's late now, much

too late to hold us back——you know that——
pay attention this time when the hiss of our names

                              ribbons off, white flame against the dark.

CLEF

At night the wind
over empty farmland

sounds like water
rolling up at me

out of blackness—
dulling the blade,

icing the plaits
of frozen grain. Once

I could sing whole arias
alone to a crowded theater

as if my own voice
could return me

to myself. I think
I was listening.

I think the white glare
of the light

is always unnerving.
When winter drops,

I see my hand
in it. A metaled fist.

My fingers fall
over pitch pine, yew

needle, furrowed bark.
So I'm sustained.

So I know all the words
for that. I belong to

a system of cleaving.
These are my papers.

See how I was a bell
clanging all night

through the broken fields?
How I spoke only in code?

I know what to do
with the dark.

Why don't you stare
through the glass.

You can witness
my rust voice, my salt

mouth. Raking up
every syllable

like sea-glass. C-sharp
is a signal. I will spell it all out.

BRUTE FORCE

I tried everything once. It was the brute force method.
For my trouble, I was kicked out of the Republic
with the other liars. I was too powerful; I intimidated Plato.

In Indiana, I walked for forty days—I stayed polite, I dirged
with appropriate pomp. On the highway, I couldn't get warm.
I burned sage & gave beautiful breakup speeches

to people who had broken up with me first. Yes, I was wounded.
I found I had strung my life between two bad men.
Helpfully, a billboard on I-65 read HELL IS REAL.

Carly Simon was like *Yeah, he probably thinks these poems are about him.*
There was a fear that I would tell the story in a way that might
unnecessarily tell someone about himself.

No one ever promised or implied that love would be
reciprocated: let's make that clear. I signed a contract
agreeing that I would not hold anyone accountable

for stealing my youth, for sending me into early cronehood.
Signature family recipes were to be withheld in talks.
Meanwhile, I turned 30. I sent a text that said

Please stop colonizing all of our mutual friends with your dick.
Cattle bones lined the trail of the dead. For five years I was fevered.
I couldn't explain how I had layered the wood on the fire.

ELEGY WITH SYMPATHY

For the bulldozed house. For the ripped-out yard. For the mourning doves that won't come back to the swamp, not this time. For the trees planted in the yard when the children are born, for how tall they grow—the trees—even after you've died so young. *Can any loved field be a churchyard* is the start of a letter I'm writing. Postmark no date. I can't bring myself to open the mail. *It's hard for us to understand God's plan* is the message, but I learned early that the flood was a sentence. An earned blight. There isn't going to be a eulogy for this. No hymn songs. No innocent dirt. For all the changeling girls who couldn't pull the splinters out, whose wings did not form. Is it a system—if the water wants to drown us—is it? If I say it's the water's fault? Behind me in the dirt there are only wet prints leading back to your grave. I don't want to take back all my trying. In the beginning there was a word for this. I carry it now like a bit in my mouth.

AUBADE WITH ATTENTION TO PATHOS

I.

Wine-drunk, ham-faced on the duvet. Cue feelings talk.

Should I have been more detached? Should I not have draped myself
on the heat vent wearing only my socks—like so?

Because he addressed me always by both names. Cooked for me when I wouldn't eat.

Making Thanksgiving food for himself in October. Patron saint of the head start.
With his dog who spoke English, possibly other languages.

Trailing a red robe in the kitchen like he was waiting for coronation.

If I loved someone like that. A figure of questionable authority
figuring out which relics to preserve under cling wrap.

For the way he smelled like cedar. Mispronounced the names of plants.

II.

There's an airport & then there's The Airport
From Which He Called Me On Our Second Anniversary
To Say He Couldn't Love Me & Would Never Marry Me Ever.
At some gate there's a specifically culpable airplane he was on for 12 hours, no contact.

There's another woman & then there's The Woman
I Knew He Would Leave Me For, there in a hotel with him—
there to soothe him, to believe, as I did, in redemptive sadness.

There's regret & then there's being so angry at myself
that I drove all night until I found the water & walked into it, March lakewater

gray & stinging. Muscovy ducks in the shallows, their strange low muttering.

III.

What is this impulse in me to worship & crucify
        anyone who leaves me—

I have tried to frame up the cavalry in gravel,
        in rectangles, in an honor code

of stamping out the fire. I'm paying attention. Look.
        There's an exchange rate

for bad behavior. It begins with the word *until*.
        I agreed to affirm small kindnesses

until disaster. A risk I could keep now & pay for eventually.
        A contract that begets blame begets

guilt. I had to say at every stage *I give permission to be hurt*. Until.
        Once he agreed to stay the night with me

& by morning a small ding in the glass had spidered over
        his windshield. The cold shattering it completely.

It's not anyone's fault that this world is full of omens.
        By all accounts, history is a practice

of ignoring things & hoping for the best. You can drive
        yourself crazy with looking. You can expect

bad luck to mark you unfooled, fooled.
        Light to mark you with light.

IV.

I know in this system I am not blameless.

          I used to promise myself

that when we broke up I would tell him

          I love you. I thought of it as a punishment.

I dreamed I let him look for me in the woods.

          I stayed perfectly quiet. I was covered in rough scales

& my eyelashes dropped burrs when I blinked.

          In the dirt below I watched him search for me.

He said *Is it enough that I want to be different.*

          Maple seeds spun out from my hair.

V.

I divorce thee, history
of looking at him in the fog
coming up over Scotland.

I divorce thee, North Sea
longing by boat.

I divorce thee, insomnia.
I divorce me driving to him
five hours over ice

& then picking a fight.
I divorce him introducing himself

as my friend, never wanting to be
on the phone; I divorce thee,
roasting pan & HGTV, I divorce

staying quiet willing him
to speak. Music for saying things

I wanted to ignore.
Anguish—I divorce thee.
I divorce thee, I divorce thee whole heart:

from the wingbone of a vulture,
I've made you a harp.

FIGURE OF WOMAN COMING OUT OF A WALL

& so it is, having slain the dragon Winter, I come to walk
the herringbone floorboards & the wet stairs of a nursing home
    out to the hall. Every day for a month I've said the words *He left me.*
At a wedding where I was happy for the couple, I declined to give the toast.

    I took his namecard from the table & told myself it wasn't stealing—
that this name I loved belonged to me. At least.
    Through the window of the nursing home, I can see the gutter dripping.
I stand taller than the wingspan of a heron to suggest I'm an arrow. Which I point.

    My grandmother, my namesake, doesn't always remember our name.
Can you say how old you are I ask & she says *Yes. December.*
    What she remembers as clear as yesterday is 1931,
standing on the back porch of the house on Roscoe with her five siblings

    watching their father burn down the garage for the insurance money.
I'm learning how to speak to her as if she could be any age.
    She thinks it's my aunt's birthday, that we have eaten *gołumpki*
& set out the cake knife & we're waiting for my grandpa, dead in 1987,

    to rummage through the cabinets for the good floral plates.
An old man in a wheelchair pulls himself by his feet along the corridor
    of Polish last names & he says to me *What's your name, little girl*
& I push through the door to stand out in the yard.

    Things are supposed to be fine now, because March
has melted five blizzards down to floods, has shown the cold no mercy.
    Coarse sleet is evicted, rainwater is raising blue tin in my veins
but I stand by a birch tree determined to speak—

    I have practiced the clock tongue. Years are erasing. This
is how time passes: my grandmother falls, Winter. He doesn't come back

for me, Winter. What was it the settlers expected
when they night-rowed their way up this flooded black river—

was it, friends, the same bullshit? Again & again that law
of starting over: spring anyway. So spring. I know that story.
     I've been holding my own arms up & I can't remember why.
There's a parquet star on the floor. The moon is losing blood.

     When I cradle the skull of a vulture to my cheek, I remember
how once I was near-bride at the not-altar, how she sewed me a blue marriage quilt
     & a dress, how I practiced holding up my face to his, certain—
because I thought saying *Yes* first was the point.

ELEGY WITH RABBITS

I need to remember how to be a body, more than a chalk outline filled in with cedar shavings, doubt. I am not buried with you in the winter ground. Observe the lifeline on my left palm, how it wings out, how it bifurcates. The cadence of my body walking forward could be *To Prove To Prove To Prove*. All the mold I remember in hindsight. Fragile as I am, I feel divided by the shadow of a windmill rolling over a cornfield. To stand up & leave behind a life. Imagine how the match strikes, how a trashpile of blackbirds is consumed in paper & ashes, paper ashes. To explain: I can't explain. I am paranoid about how much grief a tree can witness. That these woods grow older & never break their silence seems unfeeling. When I look back I see my skin shedding gray & red as it tunnels behind me. I don't want anyone to cut it away from my heel. Rabbits on the lake road hold still as I approach. Predator I have never been. I don't know what to do with my hands. But I travel with a wrongness any animal can see coming. If I startle these rabbits, I could stop their hearts—they could die of that shock. Or I may disappear the moment they stop looking. I'm breathing still. I wait for them to blink.

[EURYDICE]

Eurydice the tree is full of cicadas I hear them building their city of wet glass
hissing at night when the tree moves like hair when thousands of their bodies
pulse in the low-lit humid air pink in the streetlight when the first drops hit
& the line of rain follows like a wall of birds, walls off the whole bird-heavy sky.

There comes a point when you have to hold the man responsible for what he did.
I have decided it's degrading to say *I let him*. I say my name into the open cellar
covering my eyes. I will lead myself out of it. A tree falls over my door but I don't
touch it. I never could convince myself that the shell of those insects is only a shell.

After nine days of rain I don't walk alone in the fields I don't pick up the phone
when he calls me. How will I know myself? Hell-bitten—shade? He says *I love only you*
& every time a woman I know disappears down the long hallway of a bar with him I do not
say to her *Couldn't you trust me that if the man could stand to be loved I would have done it?*

Come out into the new wet earth pull the leaves away from your skin Eurydice.
Ivy on the linden tree. River of pale trash rolling down Asher hill. Gutter flood.
I'm here in the hail-trampled yard. Bright landscape—our flecked debris. It's ending
Eurydice. So I stand in my coat. We're almost a whole shadow now from far away.

ACKNOWLEDGMENTS

Thank you to the editors of the following journals, where some of these poems first appeared, sometimes in alternate versions:

The Adroit Journal, "Aubade with Attention to Pathos"

Bennington Review, "Elegy with Symptoms"

Blackbird, "Figure of Woman Coming Out of a Wall" & "It's Impossible to Keep White Moths"

Black Warrior Review, "Self-Portrait with Hawk & Armada"

BOAAT Journal, "[It wasn't about love]"

Colorado Review, "[Eurydice]"

Copper Nickel, "Dear Emily"

Crab Orchard Review, "The Brute / Brute Heart"

Crazyhorse, "Brute Force" & "[Remarkable the litter of birds]"

Devil's Lake, "Aubade with Boundaries" & "Elegy with Black Smoke"

FIELD, "Girl Saints"

Gulf Coast, "My History As"

The Journal, "In March When You Tell Me You Don't" & "I Have Read the Whole Moon"

jubilat, "Dear Katie"

Linebreak, "Rules for a Body Coming Out of Water"

Mid-American Review, "Thank You When I'm an Axe"

Ninth Letter, "Elegy without a Single Tree I Can Save" & "Elegy with Rabbits"

PANK, "Clef" & "Elegy for R"

The Pinch, "Four Hawks," reprinted in *American Poets* & *Best New Poets 2015*

Pleiades, "How to Mend a Faucet Dripping Thread"

Prairie Schooner, "Letter to S, Hospital"

Quarterly West, "Elegy with a Shit-Brown River Running through It" & "March Is March"

Redivider, "Brute Strength"

The Rumpus, "No, I Do Not Want to Connect with You on LinkedIn"
Salt Hill, "Philadelphia"
Southern Indiana Review, "Dear Ruth," reprinted in *American Poets*
Third Coast, "Elegy with Sympathy"
Vinyl, "Elegy with Feathers" & "Indictment"

I am forever grateful to Joy Harjo for believing in *Brute* & selecting it as the winner of the Walt Whitman Award. Thank you to Jen Benka & the Academy of American Poets, to the Civitella Ranieri Foundation & to the editorial team at Graywolf, especially Jeff Shotts, Katie Dublinski & Susannah Sharpless, for their insight, support & expertise.

Thank you to my family—for your love & faith in me, even when I did not have faith in myself: Mark & Kim Skaja, Melissa & Dave Koprek, Josh Skaja & Kimberly Giannini Skaja, Erin Cramer, Ellis & Hudson Skaja, Anne & Edward Skaja, Wilma & Deane Colburn, my very supportive extended family & the Wicker family.

Thank you especially to Marcus, dearest & brightest heart, for the happy life we are building.

Thank you to the brilliant & extraordinary women who have lived through the events of this book with me & loved & supported me in the long process of writing it: thank you to Katie Schmid & Stevi Williams Purdom, to Julie Henson, Bethany Leach, Natalie Lund, Katie McClendon & Rebecca McKanna & to Caitlin Doyle, Sarah Rose Nordgren & Corey Van Landingham.

To Don Platt, my MFA thesis advisor, who had a vision for this book long before I did & whose enthusiasm & careful analysis taught me to challenge myself: thank you for your kindness, your insight & your generosity—without you, this book would not exist.

Thank you to Marianne Boruch for helping me learn to laugh at myself in a poem & for "P.S., don't forget the mayonnaise."

Thank you to the incredible mentors & teachers I have had over the years: Scott Iddings, Dennis Brown, Stephen Frech, Carmella Braniger, Mary Leader, Wendy Flory, John Drury, Lisa Hogeland, Beth Ash & Rebecca Lindenberg—you have challenged me & made me consider the world differently; you have made me more thoughtful, more daring, more passionate & more disciplined. Thank you.

Thank you as well to the following people and institutions for their support & encouragement: the Purdue University MFA program, Kelli Russell Agodon & Annette Spaulding-Convy of Two Sylvias Press, Carl Phillips, Roxane Gay, the Association of Writers & Writing Programs, *Southern Indiana Review*, the University of Cincinnati Taft Research Center & the Women's, Gender & Sexuality Studies program at the University of Cincinnati.

EMILY SKAJA was born and raised in rural Illinois. She holds an MFA from Purdue University and a PhD from the University of Cincinnati, where she also earned a certificate in Women's, Gender, and Sexuality Studies. Her poems have appeared in *Best New Poets*, *Blackbird*, *Crazyhorse*, *FIELD*, and *Gulf Coast*, among other journals. She was the winner of the *Gulf Coast* Poetry Prize, an AWP Intro Journals Award, an Academy of American Poets college prize, and a fellowship from the National Endowment for the Arts. She is also the Associate Poetry Editor of *Southern Indiana Review*. *Brute* is the winner of the Walt Whitman Award of the Academy of American Poets. She lives in Memphis.

The text of *Brute* is set in Sabon Next LT Pro.
Book design by Rachel Holscher.
Composition by Bookmobile Design and Digital
Publisher Services, Minneapolis, Minnesota.
Manufactured by Friesens on acid-free,
100 percent postconsumer wastepaper.